# A prese[...]
# Aunt Matilda



*written by* SHEILA McCULLAGH
*illustrated by* PRUE THEOBALDS

This book belongs to:

Ladybird Books

It was winter in Puddle Lane.
Everything was covered in snow.
The Wideawake Mice, who lived
under the hollow tree
in the Magician's garden,
were very hungry.
The birds had eaten all the berries,
and the seeds in the garden
were under the snow.

the Magician's garden

"It's market day today,"
said Chestnut.
"I'll go to the market, and
get some food."

"We'll go with you,"
said Jeremy and Miranda.

"So will I," said Aunt Jane.

"You'll have to run
on all four feet," said Chestnut,
"or you'll sink in the snow.
You can't do that in a skirt."

"Then I shall leave my skirt
behind," said Aunt Jane.

Chestnut said,
"It is market day."

"I'm going too," said Grandfather Mouse.
"I can run very well on four feet,
if I take off my coat."

"What about us?"
asked Uncle Maximus.
"We'll bring some food back for you,"
said Grandfather Mouse.
The five little mice went out.
They set off across the snow.

The mice went out.

They were half way down Puddle Lane,
when they saw Miss Baker.
She was carrying a parcel.
"Hide!" squeaked Chestnut.
The mice all hid in the snow
beside the stone steps
leading to Miss Baker's front door.

The mice hid.

Miss Baker stopped at the door
of Miss Match's house.
Miss Match and
Miss Matilda Match
were very old ladies.
They were Miss Baker's aunts.
Miss Matilda Match loved cheese.
Miss Baker had been to the market,
and bought her a big round, Dutch cheese.

Miss Baker stopped
at the door
of Miss Match's house.

Miss Baker knocked
on Miss Match's door.
There was no answer.
"They must be out," she said.
She put the cheese down
on the top step.
She took out a piece of paper
and wrote "Aunt Matilda" on it.
She tucked the paper under the string
on top of the parcel.
Then she went on up the lane,
and into her own house.

Miss Baker
put the cheese
down on the step.

As soon as Miss Baker
was safely indoors,
the Wideawake Mice came out.
They ran on down the lane.
But as they passed Miss Match's door,
they smelt the smell of cheese.
Chestnut ran up the steps,
and the others all followed him.

Chestnut ran
up the steps.

"There's cheese in this parcel,"
said Chestnut.
"Let's make a hole in it, and see."

"Wait a minute,"
said Grandfather Mouse.
Chestnut had knocked Miss Baker's paper
off the top of the parcel.
Grandfather Mouse looked at it.
"This says 'Aunt Matilda'," he said,
in a very surprised tone.
"It must be a present for Aunt Matilda.
I wonder why it was left here."

Grandfather Mouse said,
''Aunt Matilda.''

"Let's take it home to Aunt Matilda,"
said Aunt Jane. "We can all eat it."

"Come back here,"
said Grandfather Mouse,
climbing up the steps, and
going behind the cheese.
"Now – push! Push hard!"
The cheese rolled down the steps,
into the snow.

Grandfather Mouse
said, ''Push.''
They all pushed.

The mice ran down after it,
and began to push the cheese.
The cheese rolled slowly up Puddle Lane.
It was very heavy, and
by the time they got
to Mr Puffle's house,
they were tired out.

The mice
pushed the cheese.

"It's no good," said Aunt Jane.
"We'll never get it home like this.
It's too heavy.
Let's make a hole in the paper
and eat some of the cheese.
We shall feel much stronger
when we've had something to eat."

''We must eat
some cheese,''
said Aunt Jane.

Chestnut and Jeremy
tore a hole in the paper,
and the mice began to eat.
They were very hungry, and
it wasn't long before
they had eaten a big hole
into the middle of the cheese.

The mice ate
the cheese.

The mice were so busy eating,
that they didn't hear Sarah
and Gita coming along the lane
in the snow.
"What's that?" said Sarah,
as she saw the cheese.
She picked it up.

Sarah saw the cheese.

The little mice squeaked with fright.
Sarah dropped the cheese.
The mice fell out, and
ran off up Puddle Lane
as fast as they could run.

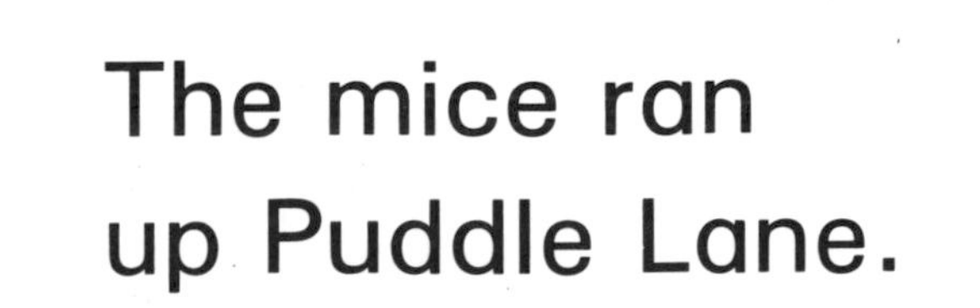

The mice ran
up Puddle Lane.

Sarah picked the cheese up again.
"Someone must have bought this
in the market," she said.
"But it's no good now."

"The mice must be very hungry
in all this snow," said Gita.
"Let's leave it for them."

"Let's take it to the hollow tree
in the Magician's garden,"
said Sarah.
"That's where the mice live.
I've seen them there."

''Let's take the
cheese to the tree,''
said Sarah.

Grandfather Mouse, Aunt Jane,
Chestnut, Jeremy and Miranda
ran back into the hole
under the hollow tree,
tumbling over each other
as they ran.
"Whatever's the matter?"
asked Grandmother Mouse.
And as soon as he had
recovered a little,
Grandfather Mouse told her
what had happened.

The mice ran back
into the hole
under the tree.

"**You've** all had some cheese,
but I'm **so** hungry,"
said Uncle Maximus.
"I don't think I shall live
very much longer,
if I don't have something to eat."

"We'll go out again,"
said Grandfather Mouse.
"We'll find something for you."

''We will go out again,''
said Grandfather Mouse.

Chestnut lifted his nose.
His whiskers twitched.
"Cheese!" cried Chestnut.
"I can smell cheese."
He ran back up the hole
to the hollow tree.
There, by the hollow tree,
was the big, round, red Dutch cheese.
"Cheese!" cried Chestnut again.
"The cheese is here!"
All the other mice came running
up into the hollow tree.

''Cheese!''
cried Chestnut.

When the moon shone down
into the hollow tree that night,
there was no sign
of the big Dutch cheese.
All that was left of it
was piled up, in little bits,
in the big hole under the tree.
The Wideawake Mice
were all feeling very full,
and very comfortable.
"It was a **wonderful** present,"
said Aunt Matilda, sleepily.
"I wonder who sent it to me?"
Nobody answered.
The Wideawake Mice were all asleep.

the Wideawake Mice
in the big hole
under the tree

# *Notes for the parent/teacher*

*When you have read the story, go back to the beginning. Look at each picture and talk about it, pointing to the caption below, and reading it aloud yourself.*

*Run your finger along under the words as you read, so that the child learns that reading goes from left to right. (You needn't say this in so many words. Children learn many useful things about reading by just reading with you, and it is often better to let them learn by experience, rather than by explanation.) When you next go through the book, encourage the child to read the words and sentences under the illustrations.*

*Don't rush in with the word before he* has time to think, but don't leave him struggling for too long. Always encourage him to feel that he is reading successfully, praising him when he does well, and avoiding criticism.*

*Now turn back to the beginning, and print the child's name in the space on the title page, using ordinary, not capital letters. Let him watch you print it: this is another useful experience.*

*Children enjoy hearing the same story many times. Read this one as often as the child likes hearing it. The more opportunities he has of looking at the illustrations and* ***reading*** *the captions with you, the more he will come to recognise the words. Don't worry if he* ***remembers*** *rather than* ***reads*** *the captions. This is a normal stage in learning.*

*If you have a number of books, let him choose which story he would like to have again.*

---

**Footnote:* In order to avoid the continual "she or he", "her or him", the child is referred to in this book as "he". However, the stories are equally appropriate for girls and boys.

*All the books at each Stage are separate stories and are written at the same reading level. Children should read as many books as possible at each Stage before going on to the next Stage.*

*Have you read these other stories about the mice?*

## Stage 1

*6* The Wideawake Mice

*13* Tom Cat and the Wideawake Mice

*14* Jeremy Mouse and Mr Puffle

*16* How Miranda flew down Puddle Lane

*17* The Wideawake Mice find a new home

*20* Jeremy's ride

## Stage 2

*8* The Wideawake Mice go to market

*from The Wideawake Mice go to market*

*from The Wideawake Mice find a new home*